NAMES FOR THE MESSIAH

Also by Walter Brueggemann
from Westminster John Knox Press

NAMES FOR
THE MESSIAH

An Advent Study

WALTER BRUEGGEMANN

WESTMINSTER
JOHN KNOX PRESS
LOUISVILLE • KENTUCKY

This book was previously published as a downloadable study titled "The Messiah:
An Adult Advent Study," The Thoughtful Christian, September 10, 2014,
www. TheThoughtfulChristian.com.

First edition
Published by Westminster John Knox Press
Louisville, Kentucky

16 17 18 19 20 21 22 23 24 25—10 9 8 7 6 5 4 3 2 1

Book design by Erika Lundbom-Krift
Cover design by Mary Ann Smith

Library of Congress Cataloging-in-Publication Data

Names: Brueggemann, Walter, author.
Title: Names for the Messiah : an Advent study / Walter Brueggemann.
Description: Louisville, KY : Westminster John Knox Press, 2016. |
  Description based on print version record and CIP data provided by
  publisher; resource not viewed.
Identifiers: LCCN 2016022698 (print) | LCCN 2016012183 (ebook) | ISBN
  9781611646702 (ebk.) | ISBN 9780664262570 (alk. paper)
Subjects: LCSH: Messiah--Biblical teaching. | Bible. Isaiah, IX,
  2-7--Criticism, interpretation, etc. | Jesus Christ--Name--Meditations. |
  Advent.
Classification: LCC BS1515.6.M44 (print) | LCC BS1515.6.M44 B78 2016 (ebook)
  | DDC 232/.1--dc23
LC record available at https://lccn.loc.gov/2016022698

CONTENTS

INTRODUCTION

For a child has been born for us,
 a son given to us;
authority rests upon his shoulders;
 and he is named
Wonderful Counselor, Mighty God,
Everlasting Father, Prince of Peace.

—Isa. 9:6

CHRISTIANS HAVE CLAIMED FROM THEIR BEGINNINGS that Jesus was the Messiah foretold in the Hebrew Scriptures. His reign began a new testament of the relationship between God and humanity. For that reason Christians often call the Hebrew Scriptures the Old Testament. Jesus did not replace or deny the expectations of a messiah previously told. He fulfilled them. The people were waiting for God to act, and many oracles in the Old Testament predicted what God would do.

What were these expectations, and did Jesus fulfill them?

Isaiah 9:2–7 is a well-known oracle, a divine utterance given to us, that uses four royal titles in verse 6—Wonderful Counselor, Mighty God, Everlasting Father, Prince of Peace. This Advent study will ponder each title and how the people understood it then, how Jesus did or did not fulfill the title, and how Christians interpret Jesus as representative of that title.

As we ponder the use of those titles with reference to Christmas and the birth of Jesus, two things become clear. First, in the witness to Jesus by the early Christians in the New Testament, they relied heavily on Old Testament "anticipations" of the coming Messiah. But second, Jesus did not fit those "anticipations" very well, such that a good deal of interpretive imagination was required in order to negotiate the connection between the anticipation and the actual bodily, historical reality of Jesus.

This book is for individual or group study.

Prayers and questions for reflection for each chapter are provided at the end of the book. Space is given for participants to write in their answers.

Week 1

WONDERFUL COUNSELOR

ISAIAH'S CONTEXT

THE ORACLE OF ISAIAH 9:2–7 IS WELL KNOWN AMONG us because of Handel's *Messiah*. The oracle did not *anticipate* or *predict* Jesus. There is no doubt that it pertained to the eighth century BCE, the time of Isaiah the prophet. While the oracle might have been utilized to announce and celebrate the birth of a new royal prince in Jerusalem, namely Hezekiah, it is more probable that it pertained to the coronation of the new king. As with the anticipation of every new U.S. president, the coronation of the new king in Jerusalem was an occasion for anticipation of a new wave of well-being, peace, and prosperity. The liturgical articulation of such expectation would have been as extravagant and excessive as such occasions are, not unlike the political speeches of promise with which we are familiar in our own political context. Included in such flowery language would have been a traditional inventory of slogans or mantras about the new king, the sort of inventory that we know from ancient Egyptian liturgies that celebrate a new pharaoh. Thus the royal liturgy in Jerusalem likely resembled coronation liturgies in surrounding countries.

Specifically, the oracle of Isaiah 9:2–7 anticipates a new regime of peace and prosperity in Jerusalem, a season of "great light" that is contrasted with the "darkness" of imperial exploitation under the empire of Assyria. The coming king, it is anticipated, will release

Judah from that oppression, and this oracle anticipates a new regime of "endless peace" with "justice and with righteousness" forever (v. 7).

"WONDERFUL COUNSELOR" = "WISE GOVERNANCE"

Our focus for the four Sundays in Advent will be to consider the four extravagant royal titles assigned to the new king in verse 6. The first of these is "wonderful counselor." At the outset it may be noted that Handel, in his famous oratorio, mistakenly placed a comma after "wonderful," thus dividing the phrase into two distinct parts. The two terms are to be taken together as "wonderful counselor" or "counselor of wonders." The term "counselor" refers to the exercise of governance, the capacity to administer, to plan, and to execute policy. God is praised for assigning a new human king who is expected to devise plans and policies for the benefit of the entire realm. The term "wonderful" may be a modifier for the noun "counselor," suggesting that the new king will have extraordinary wisdom and foresight about planning. Or it may suggest that the royal plans and policies will be of exceptional quality, a big surprise that goes beyond all the usual conventions of political power and practice. Either way it is expected that the new king will initiate policy and practice that will dazzle in its effectiveness and in its practical benefit for the subjects of the king.

In actual practice the regime of Hezekiah at the end of the eighth century BCE in Jerusalem did enact some remarkable policies, notably withstanding the assault of the Assyrian army (Isa. 36–39). In the end, however, the rule of Hezekiah proved to be a disappointment. This glorious anticipation did not work out, for Hezekiah ultimately capitulated to the rising power of Babylon (Isa. 39). Perhaps it is inevitable, given the unpredictable nature of historical reality, that such high expectations could not be realized in fact. Perhaps it is always so. That reality, however, does not preclude the ambitious expectations for the next coming king. There is always new hope when leadership changes, for example, there is excitement about every new U.S. president.

JESUS AND THE EMPIRE OF ROME

This oracular text, with its fourfold inventory of honorific titles for the king—Wonderful Counselor, Mighty God, Everlasting Father, Prince of Peace—was ready at hand for the early church when it came to bear witness to Jesus. It was, moreover, ready at hand when Handel offered his glorious work of connecting the reality of Jesus to Old Testament expectation. The expected messiah would be received as a king, and so our Christmas carols abound with royal imagery. That is, they recognized the "long-expected" king who would set his people free. As ancient King Hezekiah had to face the Assyrian Empire with its threat, so Jesus came into an ominous political situation that was dominated by the Roman Empire, with its coercive military presence and its equally coercive tax system. The royal power of "Caesar" (emperor) was to be challenged by the new Jewish king who would, in Jewish expectation, defeat the power of Rome. Thus the Christmas story of Luke 2:1–20 is situated amid the power and command of Rome:

> In those days a decree went out from Emperor Augustus that all the world should be registered. This was the first registration and was taken while Quirinius was governor of Syria. All went to their own towns to be registered. (Luke 2:1–3)

The initial announcement of the gospel in Mark, moreover, is cast in royal language: "The time is fulfilled, and the kingdom of God has come near; repent, and believe in the good news" (Mark 1:15).

The larger drama of the Gospel exhibits the way in which King Jesus takes issue with the royal power of Rome and subsequently with every regime of power that imagines it is ultimate and absolute. The power of King Jesus is intrinsically revolutionary and subversive against every repressive regime.

JESUS AS A SURPRISING ALTERNATIVE WHO EVOKED AMAZEMENT AND OPPOSITION

This leaves the early church, and subsequent church interpretation, to delineate what kind of king Jesus is. How will he oppose the royal power of Rome? In that context Isaiah's oracle provides both eloquence and substantive guidance for discerning the new rule of Jesus. The general claim of the oracle is that a new regime of peace and well-being will displace the older (Roman) order of violence and extortion.

The anticipated king who will accomplish this displacement is termed, in the oracle, a "wonderful counselor." It remains, then, for the church at Christmas to delineate how it is that Jesus is the anticipated "wonderful counselor" and what that title means for good news in the world. While royal language is often used for witness to Jesus because he is the king of the kingdom of God that is at hand, he clearly fits no conventional royal expectation. And the charge at his subsequent trial that he claimed to be "King of the Jews" rests with great uneasiness for him (John 18:34–36).

But let us consider his role as "wonderful counselor," as agent of extraordinary plans and policies for the ordering of the public life of his people.

1. Jesus Was Wise

The king as "counselor" will be wise, and so he will devise wise plans, with a capacity to penetrate beyond conventional assumptions and with peculiar discernment about how the world works and what the consequences of policies will be. Jesus astonishes his contemporaries by his capacity to see and act beyond conventional assumptions. As they observed his work, people asked: "Where did this man get all this? What is this wisdom that has been given to him? What deeds of power are being done by his hands!" (Mark 6:2).

The familiar birth story in Luke 2, moreover, moves promptly on to his childhood, when he is celebrated for his uncommon wisdom:

> The child grew and became strong, filled with wisdom; and the favor of God was upon him. . . . And Jesus increased in wisdom and in years, and in divine and human favor. (Luke 2:40, 52)

He was already then discerned, according to this testimony and memory, as being on his way as a "counselor" who would be extraordinary in his discernment. The notion of his wisdom, moreover, is extended in Paul's exposition of the wisdom of the cross that contradicts the "foolishness" of the world (1 Cor. 1:25, 27). If we consider this reference in the context of governance, being a king, then we can see that the raw power of Rome was indeed foolishness, even though it is typical for a world power.

2. Jesus Is Extraordinary

Jesus is extraordinary ("wonderful") in his teaching because he exhibited an authority that was unlike the authority of the scribes, the shrewdest and most learned of his contemporaries (Mark 1:22).

> And all who heard him were amazed at his understanding and his answers. When his parents saw him they were astonished. (Luke 2:47–48)

His teaching contradicted all usual assumptions. His teaching confounded the authorities; he engaged the powerless crowds, as he articulated a world under "alternative governance" that did not conform to old patterns of abuse and exploitation. Thus it becomes a mantra of response to his subversive testimony:

> They were astounded at his teaching, for he taught as one having authority, and not as the scribes. (Mark 1:22)

> "It is easier for a camel to go through the eye of a needle than for someone who is rich to enter the kingdom of God." They were greatly astounded and said to one another, "Then who can be saved?" Jesus looked at them and said, "For mortals it is impossible, but not for God; for God all things are possible." (10:25–27)

The terms "possible" and "impossible" contain echoes of the old question posed in Genesis 18:14: "Is anything too wonderful for the LORD?" The term "wonderful," moreover, is the same word used in the prophetic oracle, "wonderful counselor." Thus the teaching of Jesus attests to the possibility of God that the world has long since taken to be impossible. That is what is wonderful about his teaching.

His teaching evidenced a kind of wisdom that was unusual. He is wise beyond explanation! For that reason he constitutes an immense threat to conventional learning and conventional power. Thus his story of the Good Samaritan (Luke 10:25–37) or of the two sons (15:11–32) or of the workers who came late and received equal pay (Matt. 20:1–16) contradicted common practice in elemental and unmistakable ways. He is wonderful in his teaching because he opens up new possibilities that were thought to be impossible. The foolish rulers of the age did not want such impossi-

> ... the teaching of Jesus attests to the possibility of God that the world has long since taken to be impossible. That is what is wonderful about his teaching.

bilities to become possible, for such possibilities would override and displace all present power arrangements and all current distribution of resources.

3. Jesus' Teaching and Actions Display Inexplicable Wisdom

It is evident, moreover, that as his teaching was marked by inexplicable wisdom, so his actions were astonishing; he accomplished deeds of rescue and restoration that ordinary reason had declared impossible. Thus in Mark 7:31–35 he deals with "a deaf man who had an impediment in his speech." He "put his fingers into his ears, and he spat and touched his tongue," and the man was healed. And the observers of his action responded: "He has done everything well; he even makes the deaf to hear and the mute to speak" (v. 37).

From such particular cases of "wonderful," the gospel tradition can generalize:

> "Go and tell John what you have seen and heard: the blind receive their sight, the lame walk, the lepers are cleansed, the deaf hear, the dead are raised, the poor have good news brought to them." (Luke 7:22)

The old limits of the possible have been exposed as fraudulent inventions designed to keep the powerless in their places. Jesus violates such invented limitations and opens the world to the impossible. He ends that defiant declaration with the admonition: "And blessed is anyone who takes no offense at me" (v. 23).

Of course the stories of Jesus show that those who "take offense" are the elite leaders who have articulated the possible in a particular way; they have persuaded the common folk that their own definition of the possible is correct. But now they have been exposed. They will strike back, in their foolishness, to halt such "wonderful counsel."

4. Jesus Threatened the Established Order

The capacity of Jesus for the wonderful—the impossible—constituted an immediate threat to all established power arrangements. He is promptly seen to be dangerously subversive because he challenges and contradicts all normal assumptions. This is a king who refuses to accept conventional notions of governance. Indeed, he inverts power arrangements just as his mother, Mary, anticipated:

> he has scattered the proud in the thoughts of
>   their hearts.
> He has brought down the powerful from their
>   thrones,
>   and lifted up the lowly;

> he has filled the hungry with good things,
>   and sent the rich away empty.
>
>   Luke 1:51–53

Her song is an anticipation of what will fol-
low in the Gospel narrative. It is no wonder that
the authorities promptly took counsel about
how to destroy Jesus. They rightly perceived
that his transformative capacity—in subversive
teaching and in revolutionary action—entailed
the end of their dominance. Luke clearly states
the profound contradiction that Jesus' teaching
and action provoked:

> Every day he was teaching in the temple. The
> chief priests, the scribes, and the leaders of
> the people kept looking for a way to kill him;
> but they did not find anything they could do,
> for all the people were spellbound by what
> they heard. (19:47–48)

One might imagine that the authorities
judged that Jesus was conducting class warfare
by making visible the contrast between the leaders and the crowd in order to invite the crowd
into new social possibility. The crowd, posi-
tioned before established order, welcomed his

alternative. Thus the subsequent charge against him was that he was "perverting the people" (23:14), talking them out of their allegiance to entrenched order. He is indeed a ruler of the impossible!

5. Jesus Invited Followers to Continue His Mission

Before he finishes, this wise, transformative "king" will summon his followers to continue his way of subversive astonishment and transformation in the world. He anticipates that his followers, the ones who sign on for his alternative regime, will be seen as troublemakers who will seek alternatives to conventional power arrangements. That discipleship, moreover, will be the cause of arrest and persecution. According to Luke, Jesus assures his followers:

> "But before all this occurs, they will arrest you and persecute you; they will hand you over to synagogues and prisons, and you will be brought before kings and governors because of my name. This will give you an opportunity to testify. So make up your minds not to

prepare your defense in advance; for I will give you words and a wisdom that none of your opponents will be able to withstand or contradict." (21:12–15)

There cannot be any doubt that in this statement Luke has in purview the ongoing witness of the early church in the book of Acts. The apostles who witness to the transformative, life-giving power of Jesus are indeed called before the authorities. They, like Jesus, turn the world upside down (Acts 17:6).

CONCLUSION

It turns out that recognition of this new king is not just a Christmas Eve lark. It constitutes a new vocation. It is not only an acknowledgment of his new rule in the world but a recruitment for action congruent with the new regime. The "increase of his government" will not be by supernatural imposition or by royal fiat. Instead, it will come

It requires an uncommon wisdom to interrupt the foolish practice of business as usual.

about through the daily intentional engagement of his subjects, who are so astonished by his wonder that they no longer subscribe to the old order of power and truth that turns out to be, in the long run, only debilitating fraudulence. It requires an uncommon wisdom to interrupt the foolish practice of business as usual.

Week 2

MIGHTY GOD

INTRODUCTION

THIS WEEK WE CONTINUE REFLECTING ON THE ROYAL oracle of Isaiah 9:2–7 as it pertains to Jesus. We have seen how royal titles from an ancient liturgy were taken up by the early church as a way to bear witness to Jesus. Now we will consider the second royal title, "Mighty God." The early church struggled to articulate how Jesus was related to God and eventually confessed Jesus as God. (John 20:28: "Thomas answered him, 'My Lord and my God!'") That formulation, important as it is, is never easy or obvious for the church.

THE KING'S SACRAL MANDATE FOR PEACE AND JUSTICE

The Hebrew Scriptures were written in a context where the king was in some sense regarded as "'sacral,'" that is, as a carrier of some of the power that properly belonged to God and that transcended normal human power and authority. Thus we may use the adjective "divine" without drawing a firm conclusion about the noun "God." The sacral identification of the king as a carrier of "divine power" indicated that the king bore responsibility for the prospering of the entire realm that would be marked by *shalom*. Thus an effective king would assure that his realm would be marked by victory in war, by success in economics, by productivity in agriculture, and by justice in social relations.

The biblical requirements of Israel, moreover, provided that the king must practice economic justice toward the poor and needy:

> May he judge your people with righteousness,
>> and your poor with justice.
>
> . . . .
>
> May he defend the cause of the poor of the
>> people,
>> give deliverance to the needy,
>> and crush the oppressor.
>
> . . . .
>
> For he delivers the needy when they call,
>> the poor and those who have no helper.
> He has pity on the weak and the needy,
>> and saves the lives of the needy.
> From oppression and violence he redeems
>> their life;
>> and precious is their blood in his sight.
>
> Ps. 72:2, 4, 12–14

But even with this royal performance, the gift of blessing is not in the power of the king; it is in the hand of God who "alone does wondrous things" (vv. 18–19).

The modifier of our title, "mighty," bespeaks bravery, boldness, and valiance, words that tilt toward prowess in military engagement. Thus the king is identified in the oracle as one who has steadfast power to resist every threat and so to make his people safe. The king in the oracle is expected to have uncommon courage and power in the execution of the royal office, not least as commander-in-chief.

JESUS AS CARRIER
OF DIVINE POWER

When this second title is taken to pertain to Jesus, as Handel surely intends, the connection between the early testimony concerning Jesus and the title is not self-evident. Some interpretive agility is required. We may begin with the previous distinction we have made between taking the term as "God" or as one infused with divine power from God. In the first instance, Jesus is presented as one with extraordinary power and authority, but there is resistance along the way to identifying him as God. In the New Testament, it is clear that the Gospel of John will make the highest christological claims (i.e., that Jesus was God), even though much is already implied in the other three Gospels. Eventually Thomas will speak a full unqualified confession: "My Lord and my God!" (John 20:28); and before that, the man who can see after being born blind will worship him (9:38). Thus there is an acknowledgment of his divine character that will come to full articulation in the church's later expression of Trinitarian the-ology. One can see in the earlier Gospel stories that what they discerned in Jesus required artic-ulation of fresh new forms.

But the phrase from Isaiah does not first of all invite a question about Jesus' status. It asks about his power in a world that is organized around many claimants for power, most espe-cially the power of Rome. It is clear that he will not compete with the power of Rome on the terms of Rome. His assertion in the Fourth Gospel at his trial before the Roman governor is, "My kingdom is not from this world" (John 18:36).

It is clear that he will not compete with the power of Rome on the terms of Rome.

That statement, of course, has often been misconstrued as though Jesus were speaking of "another world," so that the phrase is pushed off into other-worldliness or reduced to some zone that is safely "spiritual." With this phrase he is insisting that his power is not grounded in the usual authority of empire; it is not an authority that comes out of the end of a gun or a cannon in coercive or violent ways. His kingdom, his claim to authority, is indeed "divine" in that it is rooted in and derived from "the will of the father," whose intention for the world is quite unlike the intent of Rome.

JESUS' POWER DISPLAYED IN TRANSFORMATIVE WAYS

Thus we may ask, "How did Jesus manifest and perform divine power? How did he exercise the energy and force to enact change, restoration, and new life?" Jesus exercises counter-power that refuses the coercive, exploitative power of Rome and instead enacts abundant power that makes life possible. We may focus on two episodes in his ministry that give us access to the mighty power of God that is exhibited in the life of Jesus.

In Mark 1:21–28 Jesus is confronted by a

man with an "unclean spirit." As Mark narrates the confrontation, the man himself does not actively figure in the drama. The interaction is between Jesus and the spirit. The unclean spirit immediately recognizes Jesus and sees that he is a threat to his existence and to his function of debilitation: "What have you to do with us, Jesus of Nazareth? Have you come to destroy us? I know who you are, the Holy One of God" (v. 24).

The unclean spirit identifies Jesus with an honorific title that matches the coronation language of Isaiah. He does not term him "mighty God," but he acknowledges his divine power. Jesus responds to the challenge by issuing a double imperative that asserts his authority over the spirit: "Be silent, and come out of him!" (v. 25).

Jesus (and the narrator) assume the capacity of Jesus to issue such an imperative. The spirit immediately obeys the command to come out: "And the unclean spirit, convulsing him and crying with a loud voice, came out of him (v. 26).

The spirit did not want to come out of the

man, for he wanted to occupy him. But the spirit was helpless before the lordly command of Jesus. The response of the observing crowd is an acknowledgment of his authority: "What is this? A new teaching—with authority! He commands even the unclean spirits, and they obey him" (v. 27). And then, as a result of this encounter, we are told: "At once his fame began to spread throughout the surrounding region of Galilee" (v. 28).

The crowd does not yet identify Jesus' power as divine. It only asks the question. But the question is posed in a way that implies the answer. This is the Lord of life who makes life possible for the man. Life is made possible by exercising mastery over the enemy of life.

In Mark 4:35–41, the threat is a storm at sea: "A great windstorm arose, and the waves beat into the boat, so that the boat was already being swamped" (v. 37). Jesus is unconcerned with the threat of the storm and sleeps through it. But when he awakes, he issues a terse double command to the storm: "Peace! Be still!" (v. 39).

The word is different, but it is the same command that was given to the unclean spirit. Jesus' work is to reduce the threat of the power of death, embodied as an unclean spirit and then as a storm. He reduces each of these threats to a meek, silent creature that submits to his authority. And again the one addressed, here the storm, promptly obeys: "Then the wind ceased, and there was a dead calm" (v. 39). After he chides the disciples for their inordinate fear, we get the crowd's reaction: "And they were filled with great awe and said to one another, 'Who then is this, that even the wind and the sea obey him?'" (v. 41).

In both episodes, the key word is "obey." The unclean spirit obeyed him; the sea obeyed him. Clearly the two adversaries of Jesus, the unclean spirit and the storm, are forces of chaos and death. They are agents of "uncreation" who reduced the occupied man to helplessness and the disciples to paralyzing fear.

Jesus contains and subjects these deathly, chaotic threats by creating space for new life, for the man and then for the disciples. Jesus is the giver of life who performs the function of the creator God. Thus without identifying the Son with the Father who is the creator of heaven and earth, the Gospel stories attest that in Jesus of Nazareth the early church has seen exhibited the power of God for life. It is power for life that is grounded in the creator God, for life can come from nowhere else. All the various opponents of Jesus—including Rome—are agents of death, for the empire constitutes a system of death. Power "from elsewhere," from God, is required to combat and overcome such violent force. And that power for life from God that is performed here is indeed "mighty." It requires enormous force to resist the power of death. That capacity is exhibited by Jesus so that he is indeed "mighty God," who with fearless courage takes on that "last enemy" and faces him down.

> It requires enormous force to resist the power of death.

From these episodes it is easy enough to see that same fruitful power for life in much of Jesus' ministry. Thus when Jesus enters into dispute with the scribes about his command to the paralyzed man to "stand up and take your mat and walk" or to declare "your sins are forgiven," he is exercising lordly authority that makes new

life possible (2:1–9). When he feeds the multi-
tudes, he is declaring his authority over the wilderness and recharacterizing even the wilderness
as a venue for abundant life in the orbit of the
creator (6:30–44; 8:1–10). Psalm 103 provides a
succinct doxological summary of the way of the
creator who enacts abundant life:

> who forgives all your iniquity,
>> who heals all your diseases,
> who redeems your life from the Pit,
>> who crowns you with steadfast love and
>> mercy,
> who satisfies you with good as long as you live
>> so that your youth is renewed like the eagle's.
>
> Ps. 103:3–5

It takes very little imagination to see that
in the Gospel narratives, taken one episode at
a time, Jesus is precisely performing this doxol-
ogy as a "divine hero" or as a mighty God. It
is, in these narratives, Jesus who forgives, who
heals, who redeems, who crowns, who satisfies.
It is important in utilizing this title from Isaiah's
oracle not to be preoccupied with the actual
status of Jesus (God, Son of God) but to linger
over what he actually does in specific situations.

We can see that the doctrinal conclusions eventually drawn by the church are grounded in the specificities of the stories they remembered and retold. They are indeed stories of this "Mighty God" who defies all easier categories.

ROLE OF DISCIPLES

In order that this performance of the "Mighty God" should not be "kicked upstairs" into abstraction, it is important to recognize that Jesus invites his followers to participate in these transformative acts. Early on he commissions his disciples to "cure the sick" (Luke 10:9). And they report back from their work that even the demons submitted to them (v. 17). He responds to them by asserting that he had given them "authority to tread on snakes and scorpions, and over all the power of the enemy; and nothing will hurt you" (v. 19).

That is, he emboldens his disciples to participate in the work of creation that will make an abundant life possible. In the episode of the storm, conversely, he chides his fearful disciples for having "no faith." That is, they responded with conventional fear to the threat of chaos rather than in the boldness that is grounded in the rule of God. In their fear, they flinched from that "mighty valor" that properly belonged to their vocation.

The early church is to bear witness to the life-giving power of the "Mighty God" of valor and courage who overcomes all the would-be strength of death. The beginning of the book of Acts confirms the same role for his followers: "But you will receive power when the Holy Spirit has come upon you; and you will be my witnesses in Jerusalem, in all Judea and Samaria, and to the ends of the earth" (Acts 1:8).

The early church is entrusted with the power of God. As witnesses they are able to stand before Roman authorities and attest to an alternative truth about the world. The world they describe is a world in which the divine power of healing forgiveness, restoration, and well-being is on the loose. That presence they have seen embodied in this "Mighty God." Their telling of it continues to make that power available. In the face of such testimony, the chaos of the sea and the destructive force of unclean spirits have no chance. It takes some interpretive doing, but by the end of the narrative, this little company of the faithful come to know that Jesus is the Word who is God, full of grace and truth.

Week 3

EVERLASTING FATHER

INTRODUCTION

THE THIRD LITURGICAL TITLE ASSIGNED TO THE NEWLY coronated king in Isaiah 9:6 is "Everlasting Father." At the outset it is clear that the oracle is situated in a patriarchal society in which the father is at the head of the family, clan, or tribe; exercises the most power; and has the most responsibility. To designate the king as "father" is to transfer the imagery of the family to the state, which of course suggests a hierarchical, patriarchal notion of power and authority.

The modifier "everlasting" signifies a reliable steadfastness through time and over the generations so that the phrase anticipates a reliable oversight of care, protection, and leadership. There are, in this familial domain, three things that are not surprising about the interpretation of the figure of faith in our text. First, it is not surprising that fatherly imagery, in a patriarchal society, came to be a compelling way to speak of God. Second, it is not surprising that the fatherly tasks of God were assigned to the king who is seen to be "Son of God." Third, it is not surprising that such fatherly usage is awkward when connected to Jesus, who is the "Son" and not the "Father."

ANCIENT ISRAEL'S APPEAL TO GOD AS "FATHER"

First, it is not surprising that in a patriarchal tradition the "father," as the final supervisor and guarantor of family life, should become an image for God. In this way of thinking, God is the supreme father and therefore the progenitor (creator) of all that is. Thus the early church's Apostles' Creed affirms "God the Father almighty, maker of heaven and earth." Already in Exodus 4:22 God speaks of Israel as "my first-born son," and surely it is a father who speaks. It is the same father who will later say, "out of Egypt I called my son" (Hos. 11:1). And in the extended lament in the bereft circumstance of exile, Israel will address God as father:

> For you are our father,
>> though Abraham does not know us
>> and Israel does not acknowledge us;
> you, O Lord, are our father;
>> our Redeemer from of old is your name.
>
> Isa. 63:16

And God accepts that role and anticipates that his children will not betray:

> For he said, "Surely they are my people,
>> children who will not deal falsely";
> and he became their savior
>> in all their distress.
>
> vv. 8–9

That review of past graciousness serves as an introduction for a passionate appeal to be made to God:

> Yet, O LORD, you are our Father;
>   we are the clay, and you are our potter;
>   we are all the work of your hand.
> Do not be exceedingly angry, O LORD,
>   and do not remember iniquity forever.
>   Now consider, we are all your people.
> Your holy cities have become a wilderness,
>   Zion has become a wilderness,
>   Jerusalem a desolation.
> . . . .
>   and all our pleasant places have become ruins.
> After all this, will you restrain yourself, O
>   LORD?
>   Will you keep silent, and punish us so
>   severely?
>
> 64:8–12

The father is likened to a potter, the one who decisively shapes Israel. This father God is seen to be exceedingly angry, but the assumed and affirmed kinship gives people hope that anger is not the last word. They can anticipate that the father God will do better than that. Indeed, the petition ends in some wonderment and indignation; it is unthinkable in the family that the father will not be moved to act positively. Thus the appeal to fatherly love moves the rhetoric well beyond the judicial, to familial possibility.

That expectation, that the father would move beyond anger to mercy, is echoed in Psalm 103 and anticipates God's readiness to relinquish anger for the sake of love:

> He will not always accuse,
>   nor will he keep his anger forever.
> He does not deal with us according to our sins,
>   nor repay us according to our iniquities.
> For as the heavens are high above the earth,
>   so great is his steadfast love toward those
>   who fear him;
> as far as the east is from the west,
>   so far he removes our transgressions from us.
> As a father has compassion for his children,
>   so the LORD has compassion for those who
>   fear him.
> For he knows how we were made;
>   he remembers that we are dust.
>
> Ps. 103:9–14

The notion of divine compassion, moreover, attests that the imagery ancient Israel finds adequate for God is not restricted to a one-dimensional patriarchal image. Thus, in Numbers

11:12, there are maternal images of birth, bosom, and suckling. The play on the terms "compassion" and "womb" in Isaiah 49:15 marks a motherly propensity on God's part. We may conclude that there is both patriarchal and matriarchal imagery for God; God has a motherly inclination that makes hope for mercy credible and welcome.

. . . the father God is attentive to the vulnerable and unproductive, a theological claim that is reflected in the Torah provision for widows, orphans, and immigrants. Ancient Israel is to care for and protect precisely those God is attentive to.

Perhaps the fullest consequence of God as father is the remarkable affirmation of Psalm 68:5–6:

Father of orphans and protector of widows
    is God in his holy habitation.
God gives the desolate a home to live in;
    he leads out the prisoners to prosperity,
    but the rebellious live in a parched land.

God is praised (68:4) because God protects widows and orphans, the most vulnerable in society, as well as prisoners. Thus the father God is attentive to the vulnerable and unproductive, a theological claim that is reflected in the Torah provision for widows, orphans, and immigrants. Ancient Israel is to care for and protect precisely those God is attentive to.

THE TASK OF THE KING
IS TO DO "FATHERLY DEEDS"

Second, it is not surprising that in royal liturgical theology the fatherly claims that have been elevated to be markers of God should then be drawn down to become features of the king. In general, the king is to perform the role of God in society as a regent or surrogate for God. The king is charged with the duty of pastoral justice toward the poor and the needy. This is affirmed in Psalm 72:

> Give the king your justice, O God,
>   and your righteousness to a king's son.
> May he judge your people with righteousness,
>   and your poor with justice.
> . . . .
> May he defend the cause of the poor of the
>   people,
>   give deliverance to the needy,
>   and crush the oppressor.
>
> . . . .

> For he delivers the needy when they call,
>   the poor and those who have no helper.
>
> vv. 1–2, 4, 12

Thus the royal function in Psalm 72 is parallel to the mandate to the gods in Psalm 82:

> "Give justice to the weak and the orphan;
>   maintain the right of the lowly and the destitute.
> Rescue the weak and the needy;
>   deliver them from the hand of the wicked."
>
> vv. 3–4

Like God (Ps. 82), like king (Ps. 72)! Protection of the whole family of the tribe is the work of God; derivatively it is the work of the king. For this reason the new king coronated in Jerusalem is to be the "Everlasting Father," the one who guarantees the well-being of the family, clan, or tribe, and eventually the state. The covenantal language of ancient Israel's faith recognized that society cannot prosper and flourish unless there is responsible attentiveness toward the needy and the vulnerable. The failure of kings to perform this fatherly duty can only end in trouble for all parties. Thus in the programmatic indictment of Ezekiel 34, the shepherds (kings) are severely reprimanded for failure in the royal office that has led to the scattering (exile) of Israel:

> Ah, you shepherds of Israel who have been feeding yourselves! Should not shepherds feed the sheep? You eat the fat, you clothe yourselves with the wool, you slaughter the fatlings; but you do not feed the sheep. You have not strengthened the weak, you have not healed the sick, you have not bound up the injured, you have not brought back the strayed, you have not sought the lost, but with force and harshness you have ruled them. So they were scattered, because there was no shepherd; and scattered, they became food for all the wild animals. My sheep were scattered, they wandered over all the mountains and on every high hill; my sheep were scattered over all the face of the earth, with no one to search or seek for them. (34:2–6)

The shepherd kings have not been father to Israel but have engaged in self-indulgence to the neglect of the realm. The list of royal responsibility in Ezekiel 34:2–6 is stated negatively. This is what the king has not done that is his royal duty:

- feed the sheep,
- strengthen the weak,
- heal the sick,
- bind up the injured,
- bring back the strayed, and
- seek the lost.

After the indictment, the prophetic oracle has God declare that God, God's self, will now do those things the kings have failed to do. Now we get a positive inventory:

> So I will seek out my sheep. . . . they shall feed on rich pasture on the mountains of Israel. I myself will be the shepherd of my sheep, and I will make them lie down, says the Lord GOD. I will seek the lost, and I will bring back the strayed, and I will bind up the injured, and I will strengthen the weak, but the fat and the strong I will destroy. I will feed them with justice. (34:12–16)

It takes no imagination at all to see that in a patriarchal society these are the functions of a father. Because the father-king has reneged, now the father-God will do what must be done. Only later in the oracle of Ezekiel is there voiced the prospect of a new king who will indeed do the fatherly work of kingship:

> I will set up over them one shepherd, my servant David, and he shall feed them: he shall feed them and be their shepherd. And I, the LORD, will be their God, and my servant David shall be prince among them; I, the LORD, have spoken. (34:23–24)

The anticipated king is assigned a crucial role, but it is a derivative role—prince, not king. It is as though the king (God) has in principle retained initiative and responsibility, but the prince (David) is dispatched precisely to do the fatherly work of restoration.

The kings in Jerusalem were self-indulgent to the neglect of the needy. Nonetheless the liturgy continued to hope and to function as a reminder of what is possible and what is expected from the royal office. Thus when the Isaiah oracle can identify the new king as "Everlasting Father," it anticipates that the royal office will be reliable over the course of generations in order to assure well-being. The "Everlasting Father" as king is the guarantor of *shalom* for the community.

JESUS AS "SON" IS NOT EASILY "EVERLASTING FATHER"

Third, it is not a surprise that the title of "Everlasting Father" does not work very well for Jesus, even though Jesus is the king who will restore well-being. The reason this imagery does not work for Jesus, of course, is that now it is God who is Father, and Jesus addresses God as Father. Jesus takes over Old Testament usage from the texts I have cited and identifies that title with what is likely the familial intimacy of "abba." Thus, for example, the Sermon on the Mount is saturated with Father language that refers to God. Jesus addresses God as Father in the Lord's Prayer (Matt. 6:9). It is "your Father who sees in secret" who is addressed in prayer (6:18). It is "your heavenly Father" who "knows that you need all these things" (6:32). It is "the one who does the will of my Father in heaven" who will enter the kingdom of heaven (7:21). The disciples are to be perfect, "as your heavenly Father is perfect" (5:48).

In a curious note in Matthew, Jesus challenges three titles that are to be shunned in the early church: call no one rabbi; call no one father; and call no one instructor (23:8–11). These titles were prohibited when there was an excessive hunger in the early church for status and titles. Thus we can see that Father is a title of hierarchal force that may be appropriate to God as Father but not to the Son or to anyone else.

Twice from the cross, moreover, Jesus addressed the Father: "Father, forgive them; for they do not know what they are doing" (Luke 23:34) and "Father, into your hands I commend my spirit" (v. 46).

This ready contact between Jesus and God, cast as father and son, is of course familiar in the legacy of the Trinity. The precise and careful language of the creed describes the identity and the distinctiveness between Father and Son; but there is no confusion: the Son is the Son and not the Father. Thus it scarcely works to imagine Jesus, king and Messiah, as "Everlasting Father."

None of this is surprising:

–   It is not surprising that fatherly imagery is found compelling in the tradition as a way to speak of God.

- It is not surprising that the fatherly tasks of God devolved to the royal office, the king being "Son of God."
- It is not surprising that such fatherly usage ill connects to Jesus, who is the Son who prays to the Father.

All of that seems straightforward enough.

JESUS AS FATHER IN AN "ORPHANED" WORLD

Given all of that, there is indeed a surprise! Were the care of orphans left to the Father, the Son would not be in the orphan business. And indeed, in Psalm 68, the Father takes responsibility for orphans. But Jesus takes up that task that belongs to the Father! An entry point into this awareness may be found in John 14:18, in which Jesus addresses his disciples concerning his momentary departure from them: "I will not leave you orphaned; I am coming to you."

It is not uncommon usage that disciples without their master are said to be "orphaned." But the usage stretches beyond that specificity to familial references and identifies Jesus in the role of family-making, family-protecting, family-generating father. Indeed Jesus would seem to be performing that same family-forming function in John 19:26–27 when he connects the "disciple whom he loved" to his mother: "Woman, here is your son. . . . Here is your mother."

His words guaranteed protection for his mother and fixed the responsibility of a son on his disciple. Jesus takes the role of father. If we need to justify this function in Trinitarian terms with reference to the persons of the Father and the Son, it is enough to recognize that all persons of the Trinity share all the functions of the Trinity, for which the technical term is "perichoresis." Separate functions may not be exclusively assigned to separate persons of the Trinity. But long before we get to such doctrinal formulation, it is clear that Jesus exercises familial responsibility like a father. In the Synoptic tradition, that is Matthew, Mark, and Luke, he famously said, "Let the little children come to me" (Luke 18:15–17).

And in the Fourth Gospel, he addressed his

disciples as "little children" (John 13:33). It is to the little children that Jesus gives his radical commandment in the intimacy of the family: that they should "love one another."

SUMMARY

It is, to be sure, a stretch to connect Isaiah's phrase, "Everlasting Father," to the person of Jesus. But if the father's role as "everlasting" is to stretch reliably over the generations, then Jesus is indeed the carrier of the family promises. In the conclusion of Matthew, his promise to his disciples is, "I am with you always, to the end of the age" (Matt. 28:20). In the rhetoric of Isaiah, that is a promise for all foreseeable generations. The paragraph in which Jesus utters his promise about those "not orphaned" includes an affirmation about the solidarity and identity of the Father and the Son: "Those who love me will keep my word, and my Father will love them, and we will come to them and make our home with them" (John 14:23).

Jesus is in such close identity with the Father that he shares these functions. His love commandment is to enact the solidarity of Father, Son, and community. The "everlasting" part of it is that the church, over generations, has found the abiding presence of this fatherly God to be grounds for joy, for assurance, and for missional energy.

PRINCE OF PEACE

INTRODUCTION

The fourth title assigned by Isaiah 9:6 to the newly crowned king in Jerusalem is "Prince of Peace." The king was responsible for social order and for economic prosperity. It was, moreover, understood that the maintenance of a viable social order or a prosperous, sustainable economy was possible *without* peace. For that reason, the king had responsibility to participate in and foster fruitful international relations. There must surely be some irony in expecting that the king seek peace, given the fact that fame and fortune come to kings who conduct successful war policies.

PEACE AS AN AMBIGUOUS POLITICAL CHANT

It is important to recognize at the outset that the term "peace" in "prince of peace" is the word "*shalom*" that describes not only an absence of hostility but the maintenance of a prosperous social system so that the intent is something like "promote the general welfare." Note that in Jeremiah 29:7, 11 we commonly translate "shalom" as "welfare." Perhaps the quintessential king of peace in the Old Testament is Solomon, for his very name is a play on "shalom," as is the royal city over which he presided, Jerusalem. It is clear, however, that Solomon's policies depended on heavy armaments as well as cheap labor that reflected a willingly coercive policy antithetical to "social welfare" (1 Kgs. 5:13–18; 9:15–23;

10:16–29). It is for such reasons that at his death there was open rebellion against and resistance toward such heavy-handed governance (12:1–19). Indeed, it turns out that the name Solomon is ironic, for his policies precluded any serious chance for genuine shalom in his realm.

The ambiguity of Solomon's practice of "peace" is quite at variance from the liturgically imagined shalom of Psalm 72:

> May the mountains yield prosperity for the
>   people,
>   and the hills, in righteousness.
> . . . .
> In his days may righteousness flourish
>   and peace abound, until the moon is no
>   more.
>
> vv. 3, 7

Here, in ancient Israel's liturgic imagination, the premise of peace is the practice of justice for the poor and needy, and that anticipated peace includes a more general prosperity for the people, that is, not just for the urban elites clustered around the king. In this anticipation there is none of the coercion of exploitative policies that marked the actual practice of Solomon.

The same ambiguity about "peace" is reflected in the awaited disarmament that is a prerequisite for shalom. Clearly as long as there are armaments, peace will at most be a restless, unstable possibility. And indeed, the Old Testament anticipates disarmament as a prelude to peace. But disarmament is equally ambiguous. In the prophetic oracles that are familiar to us in Isaiah 2:1–4 and Micah 4:1–5, disarmament is freely undertaken. In response to Torah instruction, those who hold arms will beat their swords into plow shears and their spears into pruning hooks, and they shall not learn war anymore!

Elsewhere, however, disarmament is itself coercive activity enforced by the victor who eliminates the arms of the losing adversary. Thus in the Isaiah oracle to which we have been appealing, disarmament is an act of violent imposition. The weapons of the defeated are burned in a dramatic way:

> For all the boots of the tramping warriors
>   and all the garments rolled in blood
>   shall be burned as fuel for the fire.
>   Isa. 9:5

And since this is in the oracle that anticipates

the king as a "Prince of Peace," it is likely that the anticipated prince of peace will be a victor who can impose disarmament on his adversaries. The same anticipation is voiced in Psalm 46, a song that celebrates Jerusalem and declares that God will end war:

> He makes wars cease to the end of the earth;
>   he breaks the bow, and shatters the spear;
>   he burns the shields with fire.
>
> Ps. 46:9

This is not a peace made by negotiation or reconciliation. It is rather an imposition by the winner. The same may be true in the peaceable covenant that Joshua made with the Gibeonites (Josh. 9:15). That uneasy settlement results in (at best) second-class social presence and participation for the Gibeonites, who must have been the weaker party to the agreement:

> "We have sworn to them by the LORD, the God of Israel, and now we must not touch them. This is what we will do to them: We will let them live, so that wrath may not come upon us, because of the oath that we swore to them." The leaders said to them, "Let them live." So they became hewers of wood and drawers of

water for all the congregation, as the leaders
had decided concerning them. (9:19–21)

This is an imposed peace in which the Gibeonites have no say.

Thus we may imagine that peace, in ancient
time as now, has a grand liturgical sound to it.
But in reality, the facts on the ground are more
ambiguous and lack the moral weight that the
more elevated rhetoric may suggest. It turns out
that peace makes a better political slogan than
a credible political reality. Thus Jeremiah can
attest to the dishonesty that operates when such
slogans provide cover for policies that are sure
to result in acute social conflict and social desta-
bilization:

> For from the least to the greatest of them,
>   everyone is greedy for unjust gain;
> and from prophet to priest,
>   everyone deals falsely.
> They have treated the wound of my people
>   carelessly,
>   saying, "Peace, peace,"
>   when there is no peace.
>   Jer. 6:13–14 (see also 8:10–11)

Hananiah, the great adversary of Jeremiah,

believed the propaganda of the royal rejoinder
(that is in fact an echo of Isaiah) and so rates as
a "prophet who prophesies peace" (28:9). The
tradition of Jeremiah,
however, insists that
such a claim is foolish
in light of the socio-
economic facts on the
ground.

It was a rare occa-
sion in ancient Israel
when the political reali-
ties coincided with exalted religious, liturgical
cadences. That rhetoric nonetheless continued
to hold out the possibility that the political reality would come to conform with the rhetoric.
The rhetoric of peace serves an important function in keeping available a vision of an alternative society in an alternative world. The tradition
of Jeremiah could anticipate such a possibility
grounded in forgiveness:

> The rhetoric of peace serves an important function in keeping available a vision of an alternative society in an alternative world.

> I will heal them and reveal to them abun-
> dance of prosperity and security. I will restore
> the fortunes of Judah and the fortunes of
> Israel, and rebuild them as they were at first.

> I will cleanse them from all the guilt of their sin against me, and I will forgive all the guilt of their sin and rebellion against me. And this city shall be to me a name of joy, a praise and a glory before all the nations of the earth. (33:6–9)

The tradition of Ezekiel can anticipate a "covenant of peace" that will be counter to the conventional exploitative coercion of the city:

> I will make with them a covenant of peace and banish wild animals from the land, so that they may live in the wild and sleep in the woods securely. . . . I will make a covenant of peace with them; it shall be an everlasting covenant with them; and I will bless them and multiply them, and will set my sanctuary among them forevermore. (Ezek. 34:25; 37:26)

And belatedly the Isaiah tradition could equate an enactment of shalom with the core announcement of the gospel:

> How beautiful upon the mountains
>   are the feet of the messenger who announces
>   peace,

who brings good news,
  who announces salvation,
  who says to Zion, "Your God reigns."

Isa. 52:7

These visions look beyond shabby historical reality. These old utterances reiterated possibilities against the facts on the ground. In the long run, the hope of faith is that vision will transform reality and the beguiling dishonesty of propagandistic speeches will be overcome. Such an overcoming would be a response to "our better angels."

THE PEACE OF JESUS AS RESTORATIVE AND TRANSFORMATIVE

In the Christian tradition it is expected and confessed that in Jesus of Nazareth the contradiction of reality and vision will be overcome, as Jesus fulfills the mandate of "Prince of Peace," that is, the "son of the king" whose responsibility and possibility is to bring peace.

In the first instance, Jesus is no prince. Loud

claims link him to David and would render him a prince. He is, however, uneasy with that title, and in any case, he is from the least of all places (Nazareth!) without any claim to a significant pedigree (John 1:49–51). More important than that, however, is that whatever claim he has to being a prince—political, not biological—he is no prince that was expected, for his notion of governance clearly contradicted the ways of governance in the empire of Rome. A "prince of peace" in the Roman Empire—or in any empire, including the U.S. empire—would be a victor who would impose peace and seize and burn the weapons of the defeated. It is, of course, impossible to imagine Jesus undertaking such violent acts as a way toward peace. Thus if we can at all apply the phrase "Prince of Peace" to Jesus, it will be in contradiction to the old expectations of the Isaiah oracle, a contradiction of the hopes of Rome and a contradiction of the expectations of such a prince of peace in the American empire as well. The peace that he will initiate and sponsor, a peace that passes all human understanding and that defies all ordinary expectations, will be a peace that is wrought in vulnerability that does not seek to impose its own way. Peace via vulnerability confounds the empire!

For that reason we must ponder the strange juxtaposition of the terms "prince" and "peace," for his notion of "peace" defies all normal notions of any "prince." For all of that, however, he does not flinch from the agenda of peace, only insisting that the peace he will enact cannot be received, interpreted, or understood in any "normal" category, that is, the categories of the empire. The following inventory from the Gospel of Luke strikes me as powerfully instructive as we consider how it could possibly be that Jesus is "Prince of Peace."

Already in the Bethlehem story, the divine messengers (angels) who announce the "royal birth" anticipate through him peace on earth (Luke 2:14). It is no wonder that the early church remembered that Herod, agent of Rome, sought to destroy him because he foresaw that Jesus was a dangerous threat to the status quo imposed by Pax Romana, which Herod supervised locally. Given the way in which the Bethlehem story is framed, the messengers (angels) make clear that this is no conventional birth and no conventional king; this is, rather, an agent of God's peace who will defy all usual categories.

The ministry of Jesus, with its narratives of miraculous transformations, concerns the restoration of the healthy order of creation. His action characteristically concerned only an individual person, seemingly without a master strategy. But these individual acts are recognized by all parties as inherently subversive and a threat to Rome. In his blessing as he dismissed transformed persons, the utterance of "peace" is much more than a simple good-bye. It is in fact a recognition that the shalom-order of creation has, in this particular case, been restored. Thus with the forgiveness of the "sinful woman," he can say, "Your faith has saved you; go in peace" (7:50). With the woman who could get no help from doctors who was "immediately healed," he issued the same blessing as he dismissed her: "Daughter, your faith has made you well; go in peace" (8:48).

As he himself wrought shalom, so he anticipated that his disciples would enact peace: "Whatever house you enter, first say, 'Peace to this house!' And if anyone is there who shares in peace, your peace will rest on that person; but if not, it will return to you" (10:5–6). His disciples are to come in peace. They are to find those who "share in peace." They are to let peace rest on those who will share. These words suggest that peace is a quite specific, personal, interpersonal transaction, so that the peace extended by the disciples is a people-to-people happening that lies beyond the conventions of imperial expectation.

Most spectacularly, in the narrative wherein Jesus weeps over the city of Jerusalem, he weeps because he knows what is coming: "They will crush you to the ground, you and your children within you, and they will not leave within you one stone upon another" (19:44). That anticipation is a clear reference to Roman destruction. But the prelude to this anticipation is an acknowledgment that it could have been otherwise: "If you, even you, had only recognized on this day the things that make for peace! But now they are hidden from your eyes" (v. 42).

The possibility of otherwise depends on knowing the things that make for peace. His terse statement here does not identify the things that make for peace. But they emerge from his larger peace-giving narrative. Peace requires the capacity to forgive. Peace requires a readiness to share generously. Peace requires the violation of strict class stratification in society. Peace requires attentiveness to the vulnerable and the unproductive. Peace requires humility in the face of exaltation, being last among those who insist on being first and denying self in the interest of the neighbor. These are all practices that mark his presence in his society.

More than that, they are all practices that contradict the conventional assumptions of empire. In the empire:

- There is no forgiveness.
- There is no generous sharing.
- There is no violation of class stratification.
- There is no attentiveness to the vulnerable and the unproductive.
- There is no humility in the face of exaltation.
- There is no readiness for being last in a world of aggressive firstness.

- There is no denial of self for the sake of the neighbor.

And of course, the empire, in its refusal of the things that make for peace, generates a society of hostility, aggression, greed, conflict, and violence. The wonder of Jesus' peacemaking is what he does in specific cases as freighted signs that break the power of the anti-peace empire. His grief over the city is an awareness that some of his own local Jewish contemporaries had been seduced and bewitched by the force of empire. It is no wonder that when he stood before the Roman governor, Pilate had no categories through which to understand him, because, as he is remembered as saying, "My kingdom is not from this world" (John 18:36), that is, not derived from fearful aggression. As the confrontation ends with a discussion about the truth, the imperial governor is left bewildered because he cannot

...the empire, in its refusal of the things that make for peace, generates a society of hostility, aggression, greed, conflict, and violence.

understand a way of truth that contradicts the power of the empire.

It is no wonder that in Jesus' resurrection appearance, when he came among his disciples, his greeting was, "Peace be with you" (Luke 24:36). Or in the rendition of the Fourth Gospel, the greeting is doubled: "Peace be with you. . . . Peace be with you. As the Father has sent me, so I send you" (John 20:19–21).

That last formulation indicates, beyond "shalom" as a conventional greeting, that his mission from God is "peace" that defies the way the world is organized. More than that, his frightened disciples are now sent by him to defy imperial notions of order for the sake of real peace.

We are drawn to confess Jesus as "Prince of Peace." We do so, however, in the awareness that this is no normal peace; the peace he brings is dangerous, subversive, and a contradiction of all that is usual. Advent is a freighted time in which to acknowledge that what we anticipate in the prophetic oracle of Isaiah deeply contradicts the expectation of ancient Israel. It deeply contradicts the expectation of those who trusted the Roman Empire, Jews, and others. And it overrides the expectations of our society, which awaits a peacemaker who will ensure our advantage in the world. The Christ child who is born, coronated, and worshiped is innocent, but he is not innocuous.

Prayers and Questions
for Reflection

WEEK 1

Wonderful Counselor

Opening Prayer

Shine your light upon us, O God, as we seek to be enlightened. By your Spirit, open our eyes, our minds, and our hearts as we prepare for the coming of your Son. Amen.

Questions for Reflection

1. What difference does placing a comma between "wonderful" and "counselor" make?

   _____

   _____

2. Jesus "articulated a world under 'alternative governance' that did not conform to old patterns of abuse and exploitation." Isaiah predicted a new regime of peace and well-being that would displace the older order of violence and extortion. Draw or describe what you imagine that world would look like today.

   _____

   _____

   _____

   _____

3. The author says that Jesus opens the world to the impossible, and this offends the elite leaders. Why are they offended?

   _____

   _____

   _____

4. How did Jesus threaten the established order?

_____

_____

_____

5. How should the church threaten the established order today?

_____

_____

_____

_____

6. As a disciple of Christ, how do you carry on this task?

_____

_____

_____

7. List something you will do as a result of this reading.

_____

_____

_____

_____

Closing Prayer

Wonderful Counselor, thank you for fulfilling Isaiah's vision and showing us that a different life-giving order is possible. Make me an instrument and active part of your alternative realm on earth. Amen.

WEEK 2
Mighty God

Opening Prayer

Mighty God, open our hearts and minds as we continue to explore ancient titles as a way to bear witness to Jesus. By your Spirit, guide us as we prepare for the coming of your Son. Amen.

Questions for Reflection

1. The author says that all opponents of Jesus were agents of death and that power from God is necessary. "It requires enormous force to resist the power of death." Name examples you can recall where Jesus resisted the powers of death.

_____

_____

_____

_____

_____

2. The author says that the statement "my kingdom is not from here" has often been misconstrued. How has the statement been misunderstood? What does the author say is its true meaning, and what does it have to say about Jesus' claim to authority?

_____

_____

_____

_____

_____

3. The author reminds readers about Jesus' commission to the disciples to "cure the sick" and his giving them this authority. Have you ever felt or practiced this authority? Describe what happened. If not, how do you imagine you could practice it in the future?

_____

_____

_____

_____

_____

4. How do you see the church displaying the power of God today?

_____

_____

_____

_____

Closing Prayer

Holy One, we give thanks for the gift of Jesus and for the ways in which he fulfills the role of Mighty God. By your Spirit, empower us to witness to the life-giving power of your might. Amen.

WEEK 3

Everlasting Father

Opening Prayer

Just as today's three Advent candles shed light, O God, illuminate our minds as we continue to explore ancient titles to bear witness to Jesus Christ. By your Spirit, guide us as we prepare for the coming of your Son. Amen.

Questions for Reflection

1. Ezekiel 34:2–6 lists royal responsibilities that have not been done by the king. Review that list in the book. How do our political leaders measure up to this list?

_____

_____

_____

_____

_____

_____

2. Exile and estrangement from God were the consequences for not taking care of the weaker members of society, including foreigners. How is our society paying the consequences for neglecting these groups of people?

_____

_____

_____

_____

_____

_____

3. How do you experience the abiding presence of a Father (or Mother) God in church?

_____

_____

_____

_____

_____

_____

Closing Prayer

Holy One, we give thanks for the gift of Jesus. We ponder the meaning of one who is the Son yet fulfills the role of Everlasting Father. By your Spirit, give us the joy and assurance of your everlasting presence. Empower us as the church to carry forth your family promises as we partner in your mission for the world. Amen.

WEEK 4

Prince of Peace

Opening Prayer

Gracious God, as we reflect on the Prince of Peace, we remember all the places in the world and our lives where conflict and death reign. Be with all who work for justice and peace and guide us to be better peacemakers. Amen.

Questions for Reflection

1. Read the chapter's introductory paragraph and substitute the word "president" for king. How well does this paragraph fit our contemporary context?

_____

_____

2. Why was King Solomon's name ironic?

_____

_____

3. The author observes that it is clear that as long as there are armaments, peace will be, at best, a restless possibility. What are the ambiguities about disarmament? What happens if those who are beating their swords into plowshares are not doing so voluntarily but rather by coercion?

_____

_____

_____

_____

_____

4. How was Jesus unlike a prince in his time?

_____

_____

_____

5. As a peacemaker resisting empire, tell how
   you live it after each of the following bullet
   points.

   –   You forgive.

   _____

   _____

   –   Your share generously.

   _____

   _____

   –   Your break class stratification.

   _____

   _____

   –   You attend to the vulnerable and the
       unproductive.

   _____

   _____

   _____

—   You show humility in the face of exaltation.

_____

_____

—   You are last in a world of aggressive first-ness.

_____

_____

—   You deny yourself for the sake of your neighbor.

_____

_____

6. Describe a world organized by peace.

_____

_____

_____

Closing Prayer

Prince of Peace, come again and organize world leaders to do the things that make for peace. Until then, empower your church to live your values and preach your peaceful realm to the world. Amen.

CPSIA information can be obtained
at www.ICGtesting.com
Printed in the USA
BVOW08s0508251116
468662BV00003B/3/P